HONEST
A
TO HONEST
QUESTIONS

Four Series of
Evangelistic Bible Studies

IVCF-Philippines Staff

InterVarsity Press
Downers Grove
Illinois 60515

© *1978 by Inter-Varsity Christian*
Fellowship of the Philippines

Produced with permission from
Inter-Varsity Christian Fellowship of the
Philippines, P.O. Box 2094,
Manila, Philippines

All rights reserved. No part of this book may
be reproduced in any form without
written permission from InterVarsity Press.

InterVarsity Press is the book-publishing
division of Inter-Varsity Christian
Fellowship, a student movement active on campus
at hundreds of universities, colleges and
schools of nursing. For information
about local and regional activities, write IVCF,
233 Langdon St., Madison, WI 53703.

Distributed in Canada through InterVarsity
Press, 1875 Leslie St., Unit 10,
Don Mills, Ontario M3B 2M5, Canada.

ISBN 0-87784-616-2

Printed in the United States of America

Preface

Even in today's world where most everyone wants everything quick and instant, people are not satisfied with pat
answers to their serious questions, especially about life and
eternity. Maybe this is because behind people's questions lie
their deep problems and needs. These are the people who
ache for honest answers to honest questions.

There is an evident moving of the Holy Spirit among the
increasing numbers of seekers who are willing to sit down and
study the Bible. Many have already come face to face with the
person of Jesus through Bible studies. And yet, many Christians are afraid to lead Bible studies because they don't know
how or don't know what materials to use. This volume of
Bible study guides is to help Christians lead their friends to
Jesus Christ. He is the answer to everyone's question and
need.

The Bible study guides in this book are divided into four
series independent of each other. Each series consists of five
to nine individual Bible studies. Each study is meant for an
hour's discussion where each member of the small group has
the chance to interact, answer and ask questions. The Bible
study guides are especially for the leader. The leader initiates
by asking questions to spur interaction and steers the discussion to cover the important points of the study. For the
leader's benefit therefore each guide is complete with a set of
questions for discussion and for personal reflection or appli-
cation. Each guide also has an introduction to the study, and
helpful notes on unfamiliar biblical terms and difficult

passages. In most studies the leader is encouraged to ask only one set of the "reflection" questions. This should be chosen in light of the flow of discussion that has just taken place and in light of where the people in the group are in their walk toward God. Many other helpful ideas can be found in *How to Begin an Evangelistic Bible Study* by Ada Lum (IVP).

Staff members of the Inter-Varsity Christian Fellowship of the Philippines have written all of these guides, except some of those in series three, "Honest Answers to Honest Questions," which were written by various students from Europe, Africa and the Middle East who are linked with the International Fellowship of Evangelical Students. A fifth series, also written by IVCF-Philippines staff, was removed from the original Philippine edition for this U.S. edition.

We are very grateful to Miss Ada Lum of the IFES who has encouraged the writing of these guides and also helped in editing. We also thank Mr. Chua Wee Hian, general secretary of the IFES for granting us the permission to print the series "Honest Answers to Honest Questions" and for permitting us to use the same title for this book. Some guides in this series are also printed in the IFES book *Jesus: One of Us* by Brede Kristensen and Ada Lum.

God has blessed the ministry of small group Bible studies on the Philippine campuses where these guides have been widely used in their original mimeographed form. May this printed volume spread the message of salvation in Jesus Christ even more widely—in homes, offices, schools and churches, to his glory.

Harvey T. Co Chien
IVCF Philippines
General Secretary
May 1978

Series **One**

Penetrating Questions from Jesus

*Jesus walked the earth with many different people:
with fishermen and rulers, pious clerics and
well-known prostitutes, rich young men and
assorted outcasts of society. But with each
he provoked deeper thinking about life. Often he
would ask penetrating questions such as, "What profit
is there in gaining the whole world
if you lose your life?" Or he'd ask questions
about himself. "Why do you call me good?" And
then there was the mind-boggling cry to
the Father when Jesus hung on the cross, "Why
hast thou forsaken me?"*

*Each of the seven Bible studies in this series, drawn
from Mark's Gospel, take up a question asked
by Jesus to help others think more deeply and more
clearly about life. It is our hope that
they will do the same for you.*

Writers: Harvey Co Chien, Melba Maggay, Danilo Noble

"Who Touched My Garments?"
Mark 5:21-34

The incident described in Mark 5:21-34 happened just after Jesus cured a man who was plagued by demons. When they left the man, they entered a herd of swine who immediately plunged into the nearby Sea of Galilee. The people there, afraid of further business losses, begged Jesus to leave the neighborhood. On the other hand, there were those who thronged around Jesus, the curious sort who would hang around anyone who smells like a superstar. And then there were those who struggled to really believe, like the woman in this passage.

Notes on the Text
5:22 *rulers of the synagogue:* Jewish society was ideally to be a theocracy, centered around the synagogue, their place of worship and teaching; and so those with religious authority were held in respect as were the civilian rulers.

5:25 *flow of blood:* A malady which according to Old Testament law made the woman ceremonially unclean and conveyed the uncleanness to all who came in touch with her (Lev. 15:25). *NBC (New Bible Commentary), 863.*

Jesus on Route to Jairus's House *(5:21-24)*
1. Before getting into the passage itself, respond to this statement, "It does not matter what the object of your faith is as long as you have faith." Do you agree or disagree? Why or why not?

2. Now read Mark 5:21-34. Imagine Jesus beside the sea with a huge crowd gathered about him. How did Jairus manage to get Jesus to go with him?

3. What actions convinced Jesus of the intensity of his need?

A Sick Woman's Interruption *(5:25-32)*
4. What interruption happened along the way to Jairus's house?
5. Look closely at the woman. What showed that the woman's case was hopeless?
6. What information did she apparently know beforehand about Jesus?
  How did she act on this information?
  What was the result?
7. Picture yourself in a crowd, people pushing, rushing, touching. What seemed strange about Jesus' comment in verse 30?
  How did the disciples look at Jesus' question?
  Why did Jesus ask it in the first place?
8. What did it cost Jesus for the woman to be healed?
  What insight does it give you about Jesus?

The Woman in Focus *(5:33-34)*
9. The woman was now put unexpectedly on the spot. How did she respond to Jesus' insistent question?
  Why do you think Jesus wanted to bring the woman into the open?
10. What according to Jesus made the woman well?
  How was her faith demonstrated?

Reflecting on Faith *(Choose one)*
11. Where does your faith lie?
  What has your faith done for you lately?
12. Faith is acting on what you know to be true. What are the things about Jesus that you know to be true?
  How, if at all, are you acting on them?

study **2**
"Why Do You Make a Tumult and Weep?"
Mark 5:35-43

Our last study whetted our appetites for this passage. Jesus was on the way to Jairus's house to heal his dying daughter when he was interrupted by a suffering woman. The woman was healed, and while he was still talking to her, some people from Jairus's house came and broke the sad news, "Your daughter is dead." We will now watch and study how Jesus handled the situation.

Notes on the Text
5:35 *Teacher:* Used in the Bible to refer to someone considered wise and knowledgeable in the Scriptures who taught the people, usually called "rabbi."
5:38 *tumult:* Commotion of a multitude especially with confused cries and uproar, typical of funeral mourning in ancient cultures.

People Asked: "Why Trouble the Teacher Any Further?" *(5:35-36)*
1. Read Mark 5:35-36. Why was Jesus now unnecessary according to some people from Jairus's house?
   How could this have affected Jairus?
2. Try putting yourself in the shoes of Jairus. How would you have felt hearing Jesus say, "Do not fear, only believe"?
   How do you think the healing of the woman just before this might have affected Jairus's faith?
3. What important elements of faith do you find displayed in his example(5:21-24, 35-36)?

Jesus Asked: "Why Do You Make a Tumult and Weep?"
(5:37-43)
4. Now read Mark 5:37-43. What seemed unnatural in Jesus' remarks in verse 39?
   Did Jesus mean that the child was not really dead? Explain.
5. What two natural reactions did Jesus bypass before he raised Jairus's daughter?
   How did Jesus raise the girl?
   What did it show about Jesus?
6. What response did this incredible incident elicit from the people?
7. What possible reasons can you think of for Jesus' strict command in verse 43?

For Reflection *(Choose one)*
8. Evaluate the kind of faith you have. Would you say your faith can compare with Jairus's faith? Explain.
   What are some hindrances to the growth of your faith? What are you doing about it?
9. Think of the most difficult situation you are in now.
   How involved is Jesus in it? How does the degree of his involvement reflect your view of him?

Note: Don't study this passage unless you have discussed the previous study "Who Touched My Garments?" They compose a unit and the progression is essential in understanding the story.

"Are You Also without Understanding?"
Mark 7:1-23

Almost everywhere Jesus went, people followed him. Some came for healing, some for deliverance from evil spirits. But still others came to criticize and attack. Among these were the religious aristocrats, the Pharisees and scribes.

Notes on the Text
7:1 *Pharisees/scribes:* Strict adherents of the law of Moses and Jewish oral traditions.
7:2 *defiled:* That which is ceremonially unclean to Jews.
7:4 *purify:* To clean, not primarily for hygienic reasons but for the removal of ceremonial defilement.
7:5 *tradition of the elders:* The teachings of the Jewish religious fathers, held to be as authoritative as the Scriptures but referred to by Jesus as the "precepts" or "traditions of men."
7:11 *Corban:* A religious pledge with payment possibly deferred until after death; commonly abused to escape the responsibility of caring for aging parents. *NBC, 866-67.*
7:21 *heart:* In Jewish thinking the center of one's being.
7:22 *foolishness:* Moral emptiness that treats sin as a joke.

Authority: Human Tradition or Divine Command? *(7:1-13)*
1. Before looking at Mark 7, list some of the religious traditions common in society today. Which do you believe actually move people further away from God? Why?
2. Now read Mark 7:1-13. In 7:1-4 what do we learn about the Pharisees and scribes? What was their reaction to the disciples' eating with unwashed hands?
3. Listen to the tone of their question in verse 5. Why do you think they questioned Jesus and not his disciples?

4. How did Jesus confront their critical attitude and implied objection? How did he expose their twisted religiosity? What was their fundamental error?
5. According to Jesus, how had the Pharisees and scribes rejected God's commandments?

Reflecting on Traditions *(Choose one)*
6. What do you think is the proper place of religious traditions? Where should they stand in relation to God's Word?
7. What family or cultural traditions (not necessarily religious) do we have which hinder us from fully worshiping God?

Purity: Outward Form or Inward Reality? *(7:14-23)*
8. Jesus now turns to the people around him, explaining further the case against the position of the scribes and Pharisees.
What according to Jesus, defiles a person?
Where is the real source of corruption? In what sense are outside, natural forces unable to really alter our being?
9. The disciples were puzzled by Jesus' statement in verse 15. How did Jesus deal with their lack of understanding?
Contrast Jesus' radical teaching on purity with the understanding of the Jews.
10. Look at the list of evil things which spring from within our hearts. How do these defile us?
What do they reveal about our true nature?

Reflecting on the Source of Evil *(Choose one)*
11. List some modern explanations of the source of evil?
How do they compare or contrast with Jesus' diagnosis?
What makes Jesus credible?
12. According to our study, do we sin because we are basically sinners, or are we sinners because we commit sins? Explain.
13. If our basic problem is one of the heart, then what solution is radical enough to change us altogether? What bearing does this have on purely humanistic efforts to change society?

"Who Do Men Say That I Am?"
Mark 8:27-33

Jesus had been performing such spectacular deeds as feeding five thousand people and restoring sight to the blind, making him more and more popular. With piercing insight, however, he knew how little they understood about his true purpose and identity. So on their way to Caesarea, he asked the disciples who he was to them and to the people.

Notes on the Text
8:28 *John the Baptist:* Cousin of Jesus. He was then a prominent figure, preaching repentance as a preparation for the coming of the kingdom and of the Messiah, the promised savior of the Jews.
Elijah: One of the prominent Old Testament prophets who, according to Old Testament prophecy (Mal. 4:5), was to return at some future time.
8:29 *Christ:* Greek for *Messiah* (Hebrew), literally, the "anointed one," the Savior promised in the Old Testament.
8:31 *Son of man:* A title often used by Jesus to refer to himself.

Jesus, Who Are You? *(8:27-30)*
1. Read Mark 8:27-30. What various views did others have of Jesus, according to the disciples?

How does this indicate the level of his popularity?
2. In turning the question to his disciples, do you think Jesus was satisfied with the people's opinion of him? Why or why not?
3. Who, according to Peter, was Jesus in the eyes of the disciples?

4. Notice the difference between the people's impression of Jesus and that of the disciples! Which, do you think, is accurate? Why?

Jesus, Do You Have to Suffer? *(8:31-33)*
5. Read Mark 8:31-33. What disturbing things did Jesus begin to teach his disciples?

How do these teachings relate to Peter's confession that Jesus is the Christ?
6. How did Peter react to Jesus' mention of his future suffering?

What does this imply about his understanding of what was involved in Jesus' being the Christ?
7. How did Jesus deal with Peter?

In what way was he on the side of people instead of God? In what sense is his understanding of Jesus' work Satanic?

On the basis of all these, does Peter deserve such a sharp rebuke? Explain.

Reflecting on Who Jesus Is *(Choose one)*
8. We often say that familiarity breeds contempt. But in the case of Jesus, his nearness elicited open confession that he is indeed the Christ. How should this affect your attitude toward a deeper inquiry into who he is?
9. If Jesus is the Christ, will it matter much how you react to him? Why?
10. In what ways does Jesus' Messiahship differ from what we ordinarily expect of a superhero?

What does it imply about the cost of following him?

study **5**
"What Does It Profit a Man, to Gain the Whole World and Forfeit His Life?"
Mark 8:34-38

Jesus taught that the essence of his Messiahship was suffering on the cross. This the disciples found very difficult to take. Like other Jews at the time, they expected the Messiah to come in glory and majesty to vindicate their national cause, setting them free from the foreign rule of Rome. And so Jesus found it necessary to teach what it really costs to follow him.

Notes on the Text
8:34 *cross:* The means used for executing the most notorious of criminals in Jesus' time. Often condemned criminals were compelled to carry the crosspiece on which they would be hung to the place of their execution. In Jewish culture, it represents the height of shame and pain (Deut. 21:23).
8:38 *Son of man:* A title often used by Jesus to refer to himself.

Counting the Cost
1. Read Mark 8:34-38. What three conditions did Jesus give those who would want to follow him (v. 34)?
How are the three linked to one another?
2. To what does the word *cross* in verse 34 refer?
What does it mean to take it up?
What did it mean for Jesus?
What did he mean it to be for his disciples? Why?
3. What does it mean to follow Jesus?
How does following Jesus differ from following a philosophy of life or a system of ethics?

Winning by Losing

4. What does it mean to save one's life?
Why is it a losing fight?

5. Explain what it means to lose one's life for Jesus.
What does it eventually save?

6. What does it mean to *gain the whole world?*
In what sense does this lead to forfeiting one's life?

7. To what future event does Jesus refer to authenticate his claim (v. 38)?

What consequence does a present decision about Jesus and life have on this future event, according to Jesus?

Reflecting on Following (*Choose one*)

8. List areas in your life where you might have to deny yourself if you decided to follow Jesus.

Side by side with Jesus' promises and claims, do the things that have mattered most to you still seem more important than him?

9. How does the knowledge that Jesus will come again alter your attitude toward Jesus and his word?

study **6**
"Why Do You Call Me Good?"
Mark 10:17-22

Different kinds of people came to Jesus with all sorts of questions. One of them was a rich young man (see Mt. 19:22). He interrupted Jesus on his journey to ask him a burning question on life and immortality—"What must I do to inherit eternal life?"

Notes on the Text
10:17 *eternal life:* Incorruptible new life in God's kingdom in the age to come.
10:19 *the commandments:* Here Jesus mentions only those commandments having to do with horizontal person-to-person relationships.
do not defraud: Interpreted as the tenth commandment. See Exodus 20:1-17.
10:22 *his countenance fell:* Deeply grieved.

An Eager Inquirer *(10:17-18)*
1. Read Mark 10:17-22. Imagine yourself being right there. How did the man in verse 17 approach Jesus?
   What would be your immediate impression of him?
   What does his question reveal about his understanding of how to gain eternal life?
2. How did Jesus deal with his question?
   Why do you suppose Jesus did not answer his question directly? What did he apparently want him to grasp first?
   How, if at all, did Jesus' definition of *good* differ from the man's?

An Impressive Record *(10:19-20)*
3. In verse 19, Jesus mentioned only the second section of the Ten Commandments. What does the young man's instant reply reveal about himself?
4. Is Jesus saying that the way to eternal life is by observing the commandments? Explain.

Why do you think Jesus did not name the other commandments?

The Missing Ingredient *(10:21-22)*
5. Look carefully at Jesus' personal response to the young man in verse 21. How did Jesus regard him?

What was Jesus' disturbing answer to his original question?

What underlying need did Jesus perceive in him?

Why do you think Jesus zeroed in on his possessions?
6. Describe the man's reaction to Jesus' answer.

Why did he go away so sorrowful?

Why do you suppose Jesus let him go without finding eternal life?

Reflecting on Commitment
7. The rich young man's encounter with Jesus obviously opened his eyes to much more than he had known about Jesus. What fresh insights did you gain about Jesus in this study?
8. What particular things in your life keep you from committing yourself unreservedly to Jesus?

study **7**
"Why Hast Thou Forsaken Me?"
Mark 15:33-39

In many Catholic and Protestant churches, Jesus on the cross is an everpresent picture. In a vague and somewhat incoherent way, we are told that he died for our sins. But this rarely has meaning and content for people today. In this passage, we encounter someone who was present at the actual scene of Jesus' crucifixion and for whom all the details of that moment gradually gained meaning and deep significance for his life.

Notes on the Text

15:33 *sixth hour:* Noon; the sixth hour of the Jewish day which begins at sunrise.
ninth hour: 3 p.m.
15:38 *curtain of the temple:* The curtain separated the innermost sanctuary from the rest of the temple. This sanctuary represented God's presence. To the Hebrew mind, the curtain connoted the utter holiness and unapproachability of God.
15:39 *centurion:* An officer in the Roman army, commanding one hundred men.

Jesus in Agony *(15:33-36)*

1. Why do you think Jesus died?
2. Now read Mark 15:33-39. Try to hear Jesus' cry.
   How did the soldiers understand the cry?
3. Do you think his cry is merely a bitter complaint of a dying, despairing man? Why or why not?
   God is described as someone who cannot look upon sin (Hab. 1:13). If Jesus is really what the entire New Testament says he is—the Savior who took upon himself the sins of the

world and died for them—in what sense has God forsaken him?

4. How many indications of Jesus' authentic humanity can you find in this passage?

Jesus—A Unique Way of Dying *(15:37-39)*
5. How did Jesus finally die?

6. How did his manner of dying affect the centurion?

Why do you think the centurion thought this as a result of the way Jesus died?

The Torn Curtain *(15:38)*
7. Besides the centurion's conviction of who Jesus was, what else was an immediate result of Jesus' death?

What can this imply about the meaning of his death from God's point of view?

8. How does this nullify the practice of having ministers or priests serve as exclusive mediators between us and God?

Reflecting on Approaching God
9. In Jesus' agonized cry, we have a glimpse of the horrifying punishment that sin deserves before a holy God. Does this explain to you the necessity for Jesus' death? Why or why not?

10. Read Hebrews 10:19-22. How does the knowledge that we can now, with confidence and on our own, draw near to God's throne affect you?

The God Who Cares

*"God does not care for this world at all," said Mario,
a high-school student. "If he does, why is this world
full of suffering and misery?"*

*Matthew, Mark, Luke and John wrote of a
man named Jesus who cared deeply for people. Once he
comforted a widow whose son died.
In Bethany, he was deeply moved by the intense
sorrow of his friends over their brother's death. And
he also wept. Another time thousands of
people listened to him until dusk. He could have sent
them away hungry. But instead he had compassion
for them. He fed them. In Jericho he did not hesitate
to eat with a much hated tax collector. (He even
invited himself to his home!) Not even a leper
repelled him. He healed one by a touch of his hands.*

*Matthew, Mark, Luke and John all say
Jesus was sent by God to sympathize with our pain and
to do something about it. If they are right, there
might be an answer to the question, "Does God care?"*

Writers: Rebecca Bondad, Dolores Girao, Flordeliza Ulan

study 1
Jesus Touched a Leper
Mark 1:40-45

Jesus started his preaching, teaching and healing ministry in Galilee, his home province. But soon he was going throughout all Israel. At first many came mainly for physical healing. Though he compassionately healed them, he wanted to solve their inner, basic problems. This we will see in the case of the leper we are going to study.

Notes on the Text
1:40, 42 *leper, leprosy:* A social outcast considered ceremonially unclean by Jews; hence Jesus' instructions in verse 44 (see Lev. 13:47-49); leprosy included other skin diseases, especially infectious ones.

1:44 *say nothing:* Jesus sternly charged the leper not to tell anyone what happened; he was getting more and more popular and he wanted to do things with as little noise as possible.

The Pleading Leper
1. Read Mark 1:40-45. What do you know about the status of lepers in Bible times?

Who in today's world would compare with lepers?

How then would you have felt as a leper during those days?

How might you distinguish a leper's inner and outer needs?

2. What do the leper's manner and actual words tell us about him?

What does he seem to know about Jesus already?

The Compassionate Jesus
3. Look at verse 41 again. Try to visualize Jesus responding to the leper's plea. Describe how you see Jesus cleansing him.

4. If you had seen Jesus doing all this, what would you have thought about him?

Reflecting on Being Like a Leper *(Choose one)*
5. Like the leper we also may have outer needs that hide our deep inner needs. Try to distinguish between your outer needs and your inner needs. What have you discovered about yourself?

How can Jesus help you?
6. What things about Jesus would I have to accept before I can respond to him like this leper?

study **2**
Jesus Said, "Do Not Weep"
Luke 7:11-17

A dead man coming back to life! What a spectacle! Yet Jesus did not do this to impress people with his power but to show his compassion for the widow.

Notes on the Text
7:11 *Nain:* Twenty-five miles from Capernaum where Jesus had just healed a person at the point of death (see Lk. 7:1-10).
7:14 *touched the bier:* Jesus ignored ritual contamination from the dead.

The Comfortless Mother
1. Why do we sometimes hesitate to involve ourselves with people who need comfort?
2. Read Luke 7:11-17. How does Luke, the author, help us to visualize the setting of the story (vv. 11-12)?
   What differences can you see between the two crowds coming toward each other?

The Comforting Jesus
3. How did Jesus feel toward the mother?
   Describe step by step how he showed his compassion for the widow.
4. Do you think Jesus could have restored life to the young man without doing all this? Explain.
5. Why do you think he became involved physically and emotionally?
   How do you think the widow felt toward Jesus when he gave her son back to her?

The Crowd Seized with Fear

6. What reactions to Jesus' actions do you observe among the people?

What kind of "fear" do you think this is? Is it like being afraid of the dark?

7. How does Luke report the way "they glorified God"?

What was the effect of the news on the surrounding country?

Reflecting on Compassion *(Choose one)*

8. What have we learned about Jesus? his compassion for people? his understanding of people's feelings?

Have you experienced Jesus comforting you in times of sorrow? How did it happen?

9. Write the names of three or four people whom you could help. What steps could you take to offer comfort to at least one of these?

study **3**
Jesus Feeds Five Thousand
Mark 6:30-44

Jesus had sent out his twelve apostles to preach, cast out de-mons and heal the sick. Then they triumphantly came back and told Jesus all that they had done. Jesus saw that they were tired so he suggested going to a quiet place for rest. They got into a boat and left—only to be met by a great crowd!

Notes on the Text
6:37 *two hundred denarii:* A denarius was a day's working wage, and two hundred denarii was possibly what the disciples had in their community treasury.
6:43 *baskets:* Used by traveling Jews to avoid eating gentile food.

The Crowd—Like Sheep without a Shepherd
1. Read Mark 6:30-44. While Jesus and his disciples were going to a quiet place to rest, what did the people do?
     What do you think this indicates about the crowd?

Jesus—The Teaching and Feeding Shepherd
2. In what different ways does the passage tell us how Jesus felt for the people?
     According to verses 34-37, what different human needs did Jesus' compassion cover?
3. If Jesus could have performed a miracle of instant meals for the masses by clapping his hands, why do you suppose he instead fed them the way he did? Trace how he worked through his disciples. What steps do you see?

The Disciples—Hungry and Disappointed

4. Now let's take a closer look at the disciples. What were they probably feeling as they reported their accomplishments to Jesus in verse 30?

How did they probably react to his offer of rest (v. 31)?

5. What kind of feelings do you suppose dominated them when they saw the crowd?

6. Why do you suppose they mentioned the late hour and the crowd's need for food?

If you were one of the disciples, would you have been disappointed with Jesus' reply (v. 37)?

7. How did they show lack of faith that Jesus could provide food for the people?

Reflecting on the Shepherd *(Choose one)*

8. Which do you identify with more, the crowd or the disciples?

9. In what ways does Jesus show concern for physical and spiritual needs?

What needs do you have at the moment? Do you feel like a sheep without a shepherd? Why or why not?

Jesus wants to be your shepherd. Would you like to trust him for your needs now?

study 4
Jesus Wept
John 11:1-5, 28-45

Death and tears are almost always inseparable. In the city of Nain, Jesus compassionately told a widow whose son just died, "Do not weep." In Bethany he himself wept over the death of a friend. Just what those tears meant we will find out in this study.

Notes on the Text
11:1-2 *Bethany:* Near Jerusalem (see 11:18, 55 and 12:1).
11:3 *sent to him:* See 10:40. Jesus was avoiding unnecessary exposure to his enemies in Jerusalem at that time (10:31).
love: The Greek word used here, *phileo,* means brotherly love, stressing affection.
11:5 *love:* The Greek word used here, *agapaō,* means divine love, stressing God's love toward people.

Some Special Friends of Jesus
1. Read John 11:1-5. Who were the three friends of Jesus in Bethany?

What do we know of Mary? Of Lazarus?

How would you describe the relationship that existed among Martha, Mary, Lazarus and Jesus? What seems special about their relationship?
2. When Jesus arrived in Bethany, Lazarus had been dead for four days. Martha went to meet him first and expressed her distress to Jesus that he had not been present to prevent Lazarus's death. After speaking with her about this he asked Martha to call Mary. Read about this now in John 11:28-45.

Trace the progression of Mary's response in verses 28-32. What did this show of Mary's regard for Jesus?

Jesus, the Friend Who Wept

3. We've seen Mary's response to Jesus. Now let's see Jesus' response to her and her situation. How did Jesus feel when he saw Mary weeping?

What does this show of Jesus?

What are all the possible reasons you can think of why Jesus wept?

4. Describe how Jesus brought Lazarus back to life.

Was it by his own power only that Jesus raised Lazarus?

How does the passage indicate this?

What then was the purpose of Lazarus's death (see 11:4, 25-26)?

Reflecting on Fulfilling Needs *(Choose one)*

5. How do you think Jesus feels when someone suffers?

What does he want to do for us when we are suffering?

Contrast this with what we usually do when we are suffering.

6. How can we imitate Mary in her attitude to Jesus?

Do you have the same intimate relationship with Jesus as Martha, Mary and Lazarus had? Why or why not?

7. His care and concern for you do not cover your physical well-being only, but also your eternal welfare. Would you like to know how Jesus can give you eternal life? [If the answer is yes, the leader may want to summarize the gospel message or give a booklet such as John Stott's *Becoming a Christian*, IVP.]

study 5
Jesus Ate with a Corrupt IRS Agent
Luke 19:1-10

On his last trip to Jerusalem Jesus passed Jericho where a great crowd was waiting for him. "Who is this Jesus of Nazareth? I have been hearing much of him lately," many people were asking. Among them was Zacchaeus, the chief tax collector.

Notes on the Text
19:1 *Jericho:* A luxurious city north of Jerusalem.
19:2 *tax collector:* Despised by their fellow Jews for working for the hated Roman conquerors; notorious for dishonesty, cleverness.
19:7 *sinner:* To the Jews, one who violated moral standards.
19:8 *restore it fourfold:* An extreme penalty imposed by the law on those compelled to pay back what they had stolen (see Ex. 22:1).
19:9 *salvation:* Entrance into God's kingdom and enjoyment of its privileges.
19:10 *Son of man:* A title often used by Jesus to refer to himself.
the lost: Those outside God's kingdom and favors.

Zacchaeus: The Despised Tax Collector
1. Read Luke 19:1-10. Describe Zacchaeus. (Look for clues especially in vv. 1-6.)
2. What did he possibly know about Jesus already?
   Why do you think he was eager to see this Jesus?
3. What was the people's attitude toward Zacchaeus?
   Why did they call him a "sinner"?

Jesus: Lover of the Despised

4. The people obviously despised Zacchaeus. But what about Jesus? How did he treat Zacchaeus?

Why did he treat him that way? (Do you think he saw a deeper need in Zacchaeus? What might it have been?)

5. How is Jesus' purpose in coming to this world (v. 10) related to his compassionate attitude toward Zacchaeus?

Zacchaeus: The Repentant Cheat

6. Between verses 7 and 8 it seems likely that an interval of time passed during which Jesus explained to Zacchaeus how he and his family could gain salvation. Whatever the message was, it was strongly convincing. What change came to Zacchaeus after meeting Jesus?

Reflecting on a Changed Life

7. You may not be a tax collector like Zacchaeus. But in what other ways have you cheated people? What can Jesus do for you?

8. So we see how Zacchaeus repented of his past sinful life. Note how very clearly Jesus himself states that this salvation has come to Zacchaeus. Have you come yet to this clear point of welcoming Jesus joyfully and personally into the home of your heart? Why? When? How?

Series **Three**

Honest Answers to Honest Questions:
Dialogs with Doubters

*Although there is no shortage of ultimate questions to
be asked these days, there is a dearth of answers.
Despite expert testimony, government studies and trips
through outer space, the only success seems to be
in finding more questions which also lack answers.
In the New Testament many people went to Jesus
with their questions. He gave answers,
but rarely the answers they expected or wanted. Let us
study these "honest answers to honest questions"
to get help not only for our questions but
also for our problems.*

*Writers: Victor Atallah (Egypt), Christopher Catherwood
(England), Hugh Craig (England), Hugh Goddard (England),
Pamela Harris (Lebanon), Werner Kromer (Austria), Gillian Martin
(England), Jo Paluku (Zaire), Wolfgang R. Wiesinger (Austria)*

study 1
"Which Is the Greatest Commandment?"
Mark 12:28-34

During the week just prior to his death, Jesus was in Jerusalem. The Jewish religious leaders had been asking him many questions to try to trap him. However, one scribe (a teacher of the law) seemed to ask a genuine question.

Notes on the Text

12:28 *disputing:* The scribes spent their time in studying and teaching the Jewish law. They would usually divide the 613 commandments of the law into "weighty" and "light" laws. There was much debate on which were the most important commandments.

12:29-31 *"Hear, O Israel . . . ":* This quotation is from Deuteronomy 6:4-5 and was the creed of Israel which would probably be recited twice daily by most scribes. The second quotation is from Leviticus 19:18.

12:33 *whole burnt offerings and sacrifices:* The Jewish sacrificial system was still in operation at this time but well before the Old Testament prophets had shown that God really wanted steadfast love much more than sacrifices (for example, Hos. 6:6).

12:34 *the kingdom of God:* The Jews looked forward to this, to God bringing salvation to his people and final judgment on those who rejected him. The Messiah was to bring this kingdom, and those who followed him would be members of it. To be "not far from the kingdom of God" means to be near the salvation God was sending.

Two Commands

1. What kinds of religious rituals or activities do people

36

consider important today?

2. Now read Mark 12:28-34. What prompted the scribe to ask Jesus this question (v. 28)?

Do you think his motive was to trap Jesus? Explain.

3. What did Jesus mean when he used the key verb *love?*

Why do you think he put the commandment to love God first?

How do these two commandments encompass all of life?

4. Why is it more important to obey these two commandments than to offer burnt offerings and sacrifices? In what ways are obeying these two commands expressions of worship of God?

5. Why did no one else dare ask Jesus any more questions?

What do you think it was about Jesus (or about the way he answered their questions) that impressed them?

Reflecting on True Worship (*Choose one*)

6. Jesus said that the scribe was not far from the kingdom of God. What do you think he still lacked?

How close to the kingdom are you?

7. People today may not be offering burnt offerings and sacrifices but they are still involved in various religious rituals or activities, such as those mentioned at the beginning of the study. How can these rituals keep us from loving God and others?

study **2**
"What Have You to Do with Me?"
Mark 5:1-20

After Jesus taught a crowd about the kingdom of God through a series of parables, he dramatically calmed a storm that threatened the disciples' lives. In this way they learned that he had authority in his teaching as well as authority over nature. They now witness another demonstration of his authority in another area.

Notes on the Text

5:1 *Gerasenes:* A region most probably on the eastern shore of the Lake of Galilee. The tombs were probably built on the ground. *NBC, 862.*

5:9,15 *Legion:* From the Latin, suggesting numbers, strength and oppression. Here it means a large group of evil forces which divided the personality of the man they possessed. Apparently they sometimes possess a person as one, sometimes as many. *NBC, 862.*

5:20 *Decapolis:* Greek name for the "Ten Cities" in the region east of the river Jordan and the Sea of Galilee. *NBC, 863.*

The Demon-Possessed Man *(5:1-5)*

1. What are some reasons for renewed interest in the occult these days?

2. Now read Mark 5:1-20. If you had been among the disciples, how would you have felt as the man approached you and Jesus?

3. In what ways did the evil spirits show control over the man?

4. What was the man's attitude toward himself?

   What were others' attitudes toward him?

Jesus and Legion *(5:6-13)*
5. What was the evil spirit's immediate reaction to Jesus as the man approached him?

What do you think was behind his attempt to enter into some sort of discussion with Jesus?
6. Why did Jesus ask the man his name *after* the command to the evil spirit to come out of the man?

What is the significance of human beings having names?
7. Why might the evil spirits have wanted to remain in that area and especially to be sent to the pigs?

Jesus and the People of the Region *(5:14-17)*
8. Why did Jesus allow the evil spirits to go into the pigs?

Some have criticized Jesus for destroying another's property. Do you think this is a valid criticism? Explain.
9. Why did the people plead with Jesus to leave their region? Why did he agree to leave?

Jesus and the Healed Man *(5:18-20)*
10. Why did the man want to go with Jesus?

Why did Jesus refuse that?
11. How do you evaluate the result of the man staying in the region?

Reflecting on a Healed Man *(Choose one)*
12. What should be our attitude to the occult?

How can we maintain such an attitude?
13. What kind of people in our community do we probably consider hopeless in their condition?

How can we learn to look at such individuals as valuable human beings?

study **3**
"How Often Shall I Forgive My Brother?"
Matthew 18:21-35

Jesus had been teaching his disciples what was required of them as his followers. One lesson concerned how to deal with a person who had offended you. Now Peter wanted this point clarified; so he asked Jesus how often he should be willing to forgive.

Notes on the Text

18:21 *brother:* Presumably someone within the community of those who recognize God as their Father. *NBC, 839.*

seven times: The Jews taught that one person should forgive another up to a third time, but not a fourth. Peter more than doubled the accepted maximum and no doubt felt very generous!

18:22 *seventy times seven:* This does not mean an exact number but implies that there should be no limit to our forgiving others.

18:23 *kingdom of heaven:* This is the same as "kingdom of God" and refers to the new society which Jesus brought into being. It is made up of those who are saved through Christ's death.

servants: These were highly placed officials in the emperor's service. They would occasionally need to borrow large sums from the imperial treasury.

18:24 *talent:* About 15 years' wages; meant to convey the idea of a very large amount of money.

18:25 *ordered him to be sold:* One way of dealing with default on debts was to sell the offender into slavery.

18:28 *denarii:* One denarius was worth a day's wage; meant to convey the idea of a very small amount of money.

Gaining and Losing Forgiveness

1. When someone wrongs you, why is it difficult for you to forgive that person?

2. Read Matthew 18:21-35. What was your first reaction to the behavior of the servant who forced his fellow servant to pay back his debt? Why?

3. Was the king's punishment of the servant in verses 32-34 justified? How so?

Why ought the servant to have forgiven the debt of his fellow servant?

4. So, summarize the character of (a) the king; (b) the unforgiving servant.

5. In this story who does the king represent?

Who do the servants represent?

What does the great debt of the servant to his Lord represent?

6. How does this story answer Peter's question?

Reflecting on Forgiveness

7. What does it mean to forgive our brother from the heart?

Who is our brother?

8. What is our situation if we don't forgive our brother (Mt. 6:12-15)?

9. Do we owe a debt to Christ?

If so, how can we repay it?

study 4
"What Must I Do to Inherit Eternal Life?"
Mark 10:17-22

As a well-known teacher, Jesus had many people approach him with their questions. In this passage a rich man (Mt. 19:22 says he was young and Lk. 18:18 says he was a ruler) wants to get a clear and precise answer about what he must do to get eternal life.

Notes on the Text
10:17 *Teacher:* Originally "Rabbi" or "Teacher of the Law"; it does not imply a strictly academic status.
eternal life: Abundant life in the presence of God; the word implies quality as well as quantity.
10:19 *the commandments:* Given to Moses by God at Mount Sinai.
10:22 *his countenance fell:* This is the only passage in the New Testament where somebody went away sad (literally "sour-faced") from Jesus.

A Struggle to Win Eternal Life
1. How important to you are the things you own?
2. Now read Mark 10:17-22. What was the man's attitude toward Jesus?
3. What does his question reveal about his understanding of how to gain eternal life?
4. What did he think about himself?
  Do you think he was proud? Explain.
5. Why was he disappointed with Jesus' reply?

A Loving but Radical Reply
6. Examine Jesus' reply. What did he mean by the first part

of his reply in verse 18? Was Jesus denying his deity? Explain.

7. Why did Jesus refer only to the commandments that concern our social relationships? Which great commandments did he obviously omit? (See Exodus 20:1-17 and Mark 12:28-34, study 1 of this series.) Why?

Divine Grace and Human Legalism

8. What do you learn from Jesus about human nature? about the kingdom of God?

9. How would you summarize in today's terms Jesus' reply about how to gain eternal life?

Reflecting on Wealth

10. What are common attitudes today toward wealth?

Do our possessions get in the way of knowing God?

What else can come between God and us?

11. On what basis can we inherit eternal life today?

Can we be sure that we have received it from God? How?

12. If we have confronted the truth about Jesus Christ and then turn away from him, what are the consequences?

"Then Who Can Be Saved?"
Mark 10:23-31

Jesus has just answered the rich young ruler, as we saw in the previous study, telling him to sell his possessions and give to the poor. But the man went away sorrowful. Jesus now speaks with his disciples who have evidently heard the conversation between him and the rich man.

Notes on the Text
10:23 *kingdom of God:* The kingdom of those who obey God and trust him, who live according to his laws. See notes in studies 1 and 3.
10:24 *children:* Students or disciples of a master; affectionately spoken.
10:30 *in the age to come:* In heaven, or the time when Jesus will make all things new.

Who Then Can Be Saved? *(10:23-26)*
1. Read Mark 10:23-31. Why do you think Jesus said it was hard for a rich man to enter the kingdom of God? Was he against riches?
2. Note that twice it is recorded that the disciples were amazed at Jesus' firm statement about entering the kingdom of God. What does this indicate about their attitude to riches?

Serving Two Masters *(10:26-31)*
3. What seems to be the disciples' understanding of the term *saved?*

Jesus did not answer the question directly. But what are the clues to his answer throughout the whole passage? See also 10:17-22.

How would you summarize Jesus' answer?

4. Look at Peter's response to Jesus' answer. What could he and his friends be feeling and thinking behind those words (v. 28)?

5. What according to Jesus is the cost of discipleship?

What does he promise to those who follow him all the way?

6. How literally do you think Jesus meant what he said in verses 29-30?

Reflecting on Salvation

7. What sort of salvation do people think they need today?

Contrast this with what Jesus says is needed.

8. What does it mean in our lives that God can do what we think is impossible?

study 6
"How Can a Man Be Born When He Is Old?"
John 3:1-15

When Jesus met Nicodemus, his ministry had just begun, but he had already made some impact on people through his miracles and preaching. Many people began to follow Jesus, but they lacked sincerity. Others were provoked to serious thinking.

Notes on the Text
3:1 *Pharisees:* Members of a Jewish religious party which was very strict in its observance of the Mosaic law and traditions.
3:3 *kingdom of God:* See notes for studies 1, 3 and 5.
3:13 *the Son of man:* A title often used by Jesus to refer to himself; a Messianic title from Daniel 7:13-14.
3:14 *as Moses lifted up the serpent:* This illustration was taken from Numbers 21:4-9.

Nicodemus, the Secret Inquirer
1. Read John 13:1-15. What facts do we learn about Nicodemus?
    Why did he come to Jesus?
    Why do you think he came at night?
2. Nicodemus, a Pharisee and a ruler of the Jews, had attained the highest position in his religion—thorough knowledge of Scriptures, rank and status with people. Now he was seeking wisdom from someone outside the establishment. What are possible reasons for his dissatisfaction?
3. What did he already believe about Jesus, according to the text?
    Observe his response at each step of Jesus' teaching. What seems to trouble him?

Jesus, the Perceptive Teacher

4. Why did Jesus respond in such a strange way to Nicodemus's opening statement?

What basically did he want Nicodemus to understand?

5. What was Jesus' main point in the illustration he used in verse 8?

6. How does his second illustration in verse 14 further clarify his teaching on the new birth?

7. How would you summarize Jesus' message to Nicodemus?

Reflecting on Rebirth

8. What are some dissatisfactions that many respectable and even religious people have?

Can you think of a specific case and consider how Jesus' teaching would apply to that person?

9. What is your religious background? How can it help or hinder your understanding of what Jesus taught about spiritual rebirth?

Do we, like Nicodemus, take the trouble to find out what the truth really is?

study **7**
"How Can We Know the Way?"
John 14:1-14

Jesus is in the middle of his "farewell speech" to his twelve closest followers. He has said that he will soon leave them; so they ask him where he is going. They are confused about what is going to happen and still do not fully understand all that Jesus has told them about himself. Jesus is fully aware that he is going to die and that he will rise again.

Notes on the Text
14:2 *In my Father's house:* Where Jesus came from and where he was returning to; Jesus is claiming that God is his Father in a unique way.
14:5 *Thomas:* One of Jesus' chosen twelve apostles, who later became known as "Doubting Thomas" because of his skepticism, especially about Jesus' resurrection. See John 11:16; 20:24-25.
14:8 *Philip:* Another of the Twelve, characterized by pragmatism.
14:11 *the works:* Jesus' many miracles of healing the sick, feeding the hungry and other demonstrations of his authority over life.

Thomas: "How Can We Know the Way?" *(14:1-7)*
1. Read John 14:1-7. How would you have felt if you had been among the Twelve that night and heard Jesus speak as he did in verses 1-5?
   What would you have thought? Why?
2. Why was it so important for Thomas to know where Jesus was going?

3. What could Jesus possibly mean in verse 3 about his coming again to take them to himself?

4. In this context what did Jesus mean by "the way"?

Philip: "How Can We See God?" *(14:8-11)*

5. Read John 14:8-11. Philip (and presumably the other disciples) did not understand fully what Jesus meant in verse 7. Yet he had been close to Jesus every day for more than two years! What seems to puzzle him?

6. What does Jesus tell them about his relationship to God?

What is revealed about his relationship to God in his statement in verse 10?

7. How does Jesus therefore answer Philip's question?

Jesus: The Results of Believing in Him *(14:12-14)*

8. Read John 14:12-14. How does Jesus further respond to his questioners?

9. What is the meaning of "greater works" in verse 12?

10. What is the challenge in verse 12?

Reflecting on Who Jesus Is

11. Compare Jesus' statements about himself with what his followers thought.

Do today's views of Jesus come closer to Jesus' statements or to his followers' views?

12. What do people today think is involved in following Jesus?

Compare and contrast this with what he says.

Do you want to follow Jesus? Why or why not?

"Do You Not Fear God?"
Luke 23:32-49

Jesus has been sentenced by Pilate, the Roman governor of Jerusalem, to be crucified. The Jewish religious leaders and the people had persuaded Pilate to do so, even though Pilate had not found a just accusation.

Notes on the Text
23:33 *The Skull:* The place outside Jerusalem where criminals were executed.
23:35 *Christ:* Greek word for *Messiah* (Hebrew); the Old Testament prophesied that the Messiah would come to establish God's kingdom.
23:37 *King of the Jews:* The Jews commonly expected a political king to save them from the Roman domination, rather than a spiritual Savior.
23:45 *the curtain of the temple:* The curtain separating the innermost sanctuary from the rest of the temple. This sanctuary represented God's presence. To the Hebrew mind, the curtain connoted the utter holiness and unapproachability of God.

Jesus Is Mocked *(23:32-43)*
1. Read Luke 23:32-43. How often does Jesus speak in this passage?
2. How does he react toward his murderers?
3. What differences do you observe between the scoffing of the rulers and the soldiers and of the words of the first criminal?
    Why does each group or person mock Jesus?
4. What is Jesus' response to their mockery?

Jesus Is Petitioned *(23:39-43)*

5. In what way does the second criminal reply to the mockery of the first? To what does he attribute his crucifixion and that of the other criminal?

6. What does he recognize about Jesus?

What is the significance of his final request?

The First Reactions after Jesus' Death *(23:44-49)*

7. Read Luke 23:44-49. What is unusual about the centurion's reaction after Jesus died?

What do you think this says about his faith?

8. Of the various people around the cross, who do you identify with most—the centurion, the multitudes, Jesus' acquaintances, the women who had followed Jesus, the rulers, the soldiers, or one of the criminals? Explain your answer.

Reflecting on the Death of Jesus

9. How would you have responded if you had been nailed on a cross beside Jesus?

10. What is the connection between the death of Jesus and the tearing of the curtain in the temple?

Who nailed Jesus to the cross—the Romans, the Jews or us?

What therefore should the death of Jesus on the cross mean for us?

study 9
"Who Will Roll Away the Stone for Us?"
Mark 16:1-20

Jesus had just been crucified, and all his followers are in a state of deep depression. They feel lost without the person who had been the center of their lives for three years. Their hope for the establishment of God's kingdom is crushed.

Notes on the Text
16:1 *spices:* Anointing the body with spices was done to keep it in the best state of preservation possible.

16:2 *the first day of the week:* Sunday; Christians observe it as the day when Christ rose from the dead.

16:3 *stone:* The sepulcher was a rock-hewn tomb whose entrance was sealed with an enormous stone.

16:5 *young man:* Generally taken to mean an angel.

16:8 Most ancient manuscripts end here. However, as verses 9-20 are consistent with the other Gospels, they will be included in this study of the resurrection.

16:11 *they would not believe:* They had forgotten his prophecies (Mk. 8:31-32; 10:33-34).

16:12 *two of them:* Probably Cleopas and the unknown disciple. See Luke 24:13-35.

16:16 *baptized:* A sign of the washing away of sins at conversion and of consequent new life from God.

Unbelieving Disciples
1. Read Mark 16:1-20. Now read Mark 8:31-32; 10:33-34. Try to visualize the women as they approach the tomb of Jesus. Try to understand their feeling of depression. But why

do you think they had this depression when Jesus had specifically and repeatedly told them he would rise from the dead after three days?

2. Why do you think they were afraid when the angel told them that Jesus had indeed risen? Compare the angel's instructions to them in verse 7 and their silence mentioned in verse 8. What were they afraid of?

3. What apparently made it hard for the disciples to believe Mary Magdalene's report about the resurrection (v. 11)?

What was their "unbelief and hardness of heart" (v. 14)?

How had they misconceived Christ's mission on earth?

What wrong picture of Christ himself did they have?

4. In spite of their unbelief the risen Christ unmistakably appears to them, and he entrusts them with the work of his kingdom. According to verses 15-16, what does he command them to do?

Reflecting on the Resurrection

5. Do people today think that the resurrection of Jesus really happened?

What is their usual reasoning?

6. Why is the resurrection of Jesus such an essential part of Christian teaching?

What are its implications for us today?

7. Why is faith so crucial (see v. 16)?

Why should we let ourselves be open to ideas that may not fit in with our preconceptions?

How should we respond if the ideas turn out to be true?

Peter, Jesus' Friend and Enemy

*If there was a disciple who professed strong devotion
and commitment to Jesus, it was Simon Peter.
From his heart and lips came outstanding
declarations: "You are the Christ." "To whom shall we
go? You have the words of eternal life." When
Jesus predicted Peter's denial, Peter promised, "Lord,
I am ready to go with you to prison and to death."*

*He was the leader among the disciples. He was their
spokesman and representative. He was the first
one to respond to the Lord walking on water: "Lord, if
it is really you, order me to come out on the water to you."*

*But this impulsive, self-confident, self-assertive
and courageous Peter was the same
Peter who sank when he saw the waves as he walked on
water toward Jesus; and what's more he denied
Jesus three times during the night of his
betrayal! Indeed, as Peter's protestations of
loyalty are the loudest, so his rejection
of Jesus is the most explicit!*

*But Jesus himself prayed that Peter's faith would not
fail. By his love and grace Peter's life
was transformed. The same promises and
transformation are free to everyone who, like Peter,
would be at one time Jesus' friend and the next
moment his enemy.*

Writers: Jane Galazo, Jimmy Ledesma, Elvira Vida

study 1
From Fishermen to Fishers of Men
Luke 5:1-11

Jesus had been performing miracles and healing many people, including Peter's mother-in-law. Up to this time, Peter had only been an observer of Jesus' miracles. But in this passage, we see him as an actual participant.

Notes on the Text

5:1 *Gennesaret:* Another name for Galilee.

5:4-5 *deep water ... all night:* The best fishing was at night in deep water; during daytime people fished in the shallow waters.

5:8 *Simon Peter:* "Simon Peter receives his full name only here in Luke (cf. 6:14), since his call was the moment which made his new name possible. He was not necessarily more sinful than other men, but he felt that fear which all sinful men ought to feel in the presence of the divine." *NBC, 897.*

A Bigger Catch

1. Read Luke 5:1-11. Why do you suppose so many people were coming to hear Jesus? Why in the face of such a crowd might Jesus have gotten into the boat?

2. What did he probably know about Simon's current problem (note v. 2)?

Why do you think he chose Simon's boat?

3. Simon obviously obeyed without hesitation when Jesus gave instructions in verse 3. But how did he react to Jesus' command in verse 4?

4. Consider the situation of Simon and the other fishermen after an unsuccessful night of fishing. How do you think Simon and company felt after hearing such a command from a nonfisherman?

Why did he obey anyway?

5. Describe the results of Simon's obedience that followed in verses 6-8.

Had you been on the boat that morning, how would you have reacted?

Why did Simon respond as he did to the catch?

6. What was Jesus asking the fishermen to do in verse 10?

What immediate decision did they make as a response to Jesus' call?

What did following Jesus involve for them?

What would *everything* include for an ordinary fisherman?

7. If you were to leave everything and follow Jesus, what would it include?

8. What attitude to Jesus did these fishermen show?

What attitude do you have toward Jesus?

Reflecting on Leaving Everything (*Choose one*)

9. What about Jesus should convince us to value him more than anything or anybody else in our lives?

What differences would this make in our studies, family relations, friendships, ambitions and innermost desires in life?

10. Take a look at yourself. What do you see? Write a short letter to Jesus telling him how you see him as you have observed from this incident and what you would like him to do for you.

study **2**
"Why Did You Doubt?"
Matthew 14:22-33

Peter has seen Jesus perform the miracle of the great catch of fish as well as the feeding of over five thousand people and other miracles. Surely now he knows that Jesus has supernatural powers. But let us see how he gets along in the following situation. The disciples are on their way to the other side of the lake, having been sent ahead by Jesus after the miraculous feeding.

Notes on the Text
14:24, 30 *the wind:* Indicating a sudden storm that even these experienced fishermen could not cope with.
14:25 *fourth watch of the night:* Between three and six o'clock in the morning.

He Said, "Come."
1. What are some fears or difficult situations you find yourself in now?
2. Read Matthew 14:22-33. After a tiring day of dealing with crowds of people, we would want to go right to bed. But what did Jesus do?

What does this say about Jesus' priorities?
3. Let us now leave Jesus in the hills and go to the lake where the disciples are. Describe their situation.

How did they probably feel? (What was their conversation probably like? What kind of facial expressions did they have?)
4. Suddenly they were even more terrified! Why?
5. How did Jesus calm their fears?

His short statement about himself in verse 27 is loaded. What did he intend to communicate?

58

6. What does Peter's action tell us about his character?

But soon he began to sink. Examine the cause (vv. 30-31).

In what ways are we like Peter in reacting to fearful or difficult situations?

7. Note how quickly Jesus reached out for Peter's hand. What did Peter realize first before Jesus saved him?

What was Jesus' fitting rebuke for him?

And what was the disciples' fitting response to Jesus?

Reflecting on Your Fears *(Choose one)*

8. Think back to the fears you mentioned at the beginning of the discussion. How does this passage indicate that you should look at them now?

9. Consider your present relationship to Jesus. Have you been personally worshiping him as the Lord of your life or has it been just a worship of a distant God? Explain.

study 3
"To Whom Shall We Go?"
John 6:60-71

The people, having been fed miraculously by Jesus, pursued him to the other side of the lake. They have come, however, for purely selfish reasons. They see Jesus only as a potential provider of their food and other material needs. Jesus corrects this view and declares to them that he is the Living Bread of God. We shall see in this study the effect of this teaching on them.

Notes on the Text

6:60 *a hard saying:* Refers to the previous discussion in verses 52-59. Taking Jesus literally, they did not understand what he meant.

6:62 *ascending:* Jesus was teaching more about his resurrection and return to heaven after his death.

6:63 *the flesh is of no avail:* Only a spiritual response to Christ's life-giving words can lead to spiritual life. Yet only the Holy Spirit can create a spiritual response to Christ's words.

6:69 *Holy One of God:* Acknowledgment that Jesus is God's chosen one to bring eternal life to mankind.

Choices about Eternal Life

1. Where do people go, who or what do they look to, to find eternal life (ultimate purpose, true meaning)?

2. Now read John 6:60-71 to see some other reactions. What was the reaction of many disciples to Jesus' teaching (vv. 60-61)? Why?

3. What did Jesus claim about his own teaching (v. 63)?

What about Jesus' teaching made it difficult for the disciples to follow him?

4. Jesus then turned to the Twelve Apostles and asked them a crucial question (v. 67). How do you think Jesus was feeling when he asked them this question?

How would you describe Jesus' attitude to the choices or decisions people make about eternal life?

5. Speaking for the disciples, what had Peter come to realize about Jesus by this time?

How did he now regard Jesus' teaching?

How do you think Peter arrived at this conclusion?

6. Jesus' words tell us who he is. How important or unimportant are Jesus' words in our lives? Give examples.

7. What did Jesus know about Judas' future choice?

In what ways could Judas have possibly given clues about his evil motives?

What do verses 70-71 tell us about the choice of a professing follower of Jesus Christ?

Reflecting on Eternal Life *(Choose one)*
8. If you were in the place of the disciples, how would you respond after hearing Jesus' teaching?

9. Where did Peter find eternal life? Where are you finding eternal life?

"You Are the Christ"
Matthew 16:13-22

Jesus was aware that the opposition against him by the religious leaders was growing stronger. He brought his disciples to Caesarea Philippi, far from the hostile religious leaders and asked them the question, "Who do men say I am?"

Notes on the Text
16:13 *Son of man:* A name Jesus applied to himself to describe his character and mission (see Dan. 7:13-14).
16:14 *prophet:* A person whom God especially chooses to *proclaim* God's Word to the people and to *predict* future events.
16:16 *Christ:* Greek for *Messiah* (Hebrew), literally meaning "anointed one." It is the official title for the expected political deliverer and liberator of the Jews.
16:18 *rock:* There is a play on words in the Greek here. The first *rock* is "Petros," meaning a stone (translated as "Peter"). The second *rock* is "petra," meaning a huge rock (translated as "rock").
16:19 *the keys:* Symbolizes the great authority of a steward rather than a doorkeeper. They are the keys of knowledge which Christ entrusts to those who preach the gospel and thus opening God's kingdom to all believers.

"Who Do You Say That I Am?"
1. Look back on our previous studies. How would you describe Jesus' relationship with his disciples at this point?

What did they already know about Jesus?
2. Now read Matthew 16:13-22. Why do you think Jesus asked the disciples this question in verse 13?

From the disciples' answers, how did the people regard

Jesus?

What did the answers reveal about Jesus' impact on the people?

3. Jesus then turned the question directly to the disciples. How did Peter regard Christ?

How different was his view from the others'?

4. What difficulties did Peter have to overcome to make this confession? (Remember that Peter was a Jew and the Messiah to them was a political deliverer.)

5. How did Peter reach this conclusion about Jesus (v. 17)?

Because of Peter's confession, what did Jesus promise Peter?

What authority did he give Peter?

6. After this recognition, Jesus was able to reveal more about himself. What did he reveal to his disciples?

What was Peter's reaction to Christ's statement?

Contrast Peter's recognition of Christ's person (v. 16) and his understanding of Christ's mission (v. 22). Jesus, in turn, rebuked Peter. Why do you think this difference existed?

What did Jesus reveal about his attitude toward his own death?

Reflecting on Who Jesus Is (*Choose one*)

7. Today, what are some common ideas as to who Jesus really is?

What do you personally think of Jesus?

How did you reach such conclusions?

8. Jesus, it has been said, is "the man you cannot ignore." Nobody can dare be indifferent to Jesus because of his fantastic claims about himself (see also Jn. 11:25-26; 14:6). Why is it important for us to know who Jesus really is?

How will knowledge of who Jesus is affect our lives?

What will happen to us if we do not truly know Christ?

"How Often Shall I Forgive?"
Matthew 18:21-35

Jesus had been talking about healthy relationships among his disciples. Specifically he had taught that if one brother sinned against another, the brother who was wronged should go and talk to him about his fault (Mt. 18:15-17). These admonitions provoked Peter to ask, "How often shall my brother sin against me and I forgive him?" a question we ourselves might ask.

Notes on the Text
18:22 *seventy times seven:* An exact 490 times is not implied but unlimited forgiveness.

18:23 *the servants:* High officials in the service of the Emperor, some of whom would occasionally borrow large sums from the imperial treasury.

18:24 *ten thousand talents:* One talent was worth about 15 years' wages.

18:28 *one hundred denarii:* One denarius was worth a day's wage.

A Story about Forgiveness
1. What does *forgiveness* mean to you?

2. Read Matthew 18:21-35. Jewish tradition taught that someone was to be forgiven three times but no more. What may Peter have been thinking and feeling when he asked Jesus, "How often shall my brother sin against me and I forgive him? As many as seven times"?

3. How does Jesus answer?

Was he being literal? If not, what does he mean by this strange answer?

4. Jesus illustrated the meaning of forgiveness through a parable. Contrast the king's treatment of the servant and the servant's treatment of his fellow servant.

What kind of person was the king?

What kind of person was the servant?

How should he have treated his fellow servant? Why?

5. What do you think Jesus was emphasizing in this parable?

Reflecting on Forgiveness (*Choose one*)

6. From this study, what do you learn about the nature and character of Jesus?

What do you learn of God the Father (vv. 22-23, 25, 32, 34-35)?

How do you respond to the portrait of God in this parable?

7. What adjectives could you use to describe the way God forgives?

How should God's forgiveness of us affect our forgiveness of others?

8. Is it possible that it is difficult to forgive others because we have not known God's forgiveness?

Have you personally experienced God's forgiveness for your sins?

What assurance do you have?

study **6**
"Satan Demanded to Have You"
Luke 22:24-34

Jesus is now less than twenty-four hours from his crucifixion. He turns his last supper together with his disciples into a symbol of his sacrificial death for humanity. However, a dispute breaks out among the disciples about who should be the greatest. Jesus then makes reference to the prevailing worldly notion of greatness and contrasts his own idea of it.

Notes on the Text
22:30 *eat and drink at my table:* Fellowship with Christ, co-ruling with Christ during a future universal reign.
22:31 *Satan demanded:* See Job 1—2.
22:31-32 *you:* Plural in verse 31; singular in verse 32.

A Debate of Greatness
1. What is the world's idea of greatness?
2. Read Luke 22:24-34. How does Jesus describe the world's idea of greatness?

How does Jesus' own view differ?

What virtue does Christ consider great?
3. What qualities of Jesus do you see portrayed in this situation which reveal his own attitude to power? to himself? to his disciples?

What attitudes in his disciples was he correcting (see v. 24)?
4. Despite their quarreling Jesus says he appreciates them! In verses 28-30 what quality in his disciples does he commend?

Because of this quality, what reward does he promise to his disciples?

5. Now Jesus turns to Simon Peter. What general impression do you get of Jesus' attitude to Peter here?

What sobering truth does Jesus reveal to him?

We don't usually think about Jesus having faith in people. But we can see it in verse 32. What did he fully trust Simon Peter to do?

What can we learn from Jesus himself about God's purpose in allowing trials?

6. How would you describe Peter's commitment from his answer to Jesus?

How does Jesus view this "loyal-to-death" commitment?

How are we like Peter?

What might it cost us to follow Jesus?

Reflecting on Consistency *(Choose one)*

7. What difference has following Christ made in your life?

8. What does Jesus demand from those who profess to follow him?

9. In what area(s) of your life is following Jesus most difficult?

study **7**
"I Do Not Know the Man"
Matthew 26:69-75

Jesus had told his disciples the sobering truth that all his disciples would run and leave him that night of his arrest. But Peter boldly affirmed, "I will never leave you, even though all the rest may." Jesus rebuked him saying, "Before the cock crows, you will deny me three times." In this passage we find Peter eating his own words.

Notes on the Text
26:69 *courtyard:* See 26:57-58.
26:70 *all:* The guards mentioned in verse 58.
26:73 *accent:* Galileans spoke with a regional accent.
26:74 *cock crowed:* Indicating the early dawn of the last night which Jesus had spent with his disciples before he had been arrested and put on trial.

A Rocky Peter
1. Jesus' arrest was a huge blow to the disciples. Not only was their Teacher and Lord gone, their dreams of God's kingdom on earth were smashed. They were discouraged and fearful.

Read Matthew 26:69-70. What is strange about finding Peter in the courtyard? What do you think he was doing there?

2. Put yourself in Peter's shoes. How would you be feeling at this time? What thoughts would keep running through your mind?

3. Who were the different people who recognized Peter?

How did they recognize him?

What was Peter's response?

What progression do you notice in Peter's responses?

How does this help you to understand Peter better?

What effect did this denial have on him?

4. Recall from the past studies all that Peter had said in commitment to Jesus. What kind of Peter do we now see here?

5. What does the fulfillment of Jesus' prediction of Peter's denial show about Jesus?

But Jesus does not have an "I told you so" attitude. Recall the last study in Luke 22:31-33. What else had Jesus told Simon Peter besides predicting his denial? What does this show about Jesus' main concern?

Reflecting on Denial *(Choose one)*

6. Have you had a similar experience to Simon Peter's when you hesitated to be identified with Jesus? Why?

Would you like to ask him now for forgiveness and start life again with him?

7. Recall experiences when you told a lie. How did you feel then?

How does lying affect us?

study **8**
"Do You Love Me?"
John 21:15-22

After the resurrection Jesus appeared many times to his disciples. Here is one instance by the Sea of Tiberias. Again he helped them with a marvelous catch of fish and prepared a breakfast of broiled fish and bread. Immediately afterward Jesus had a private talk with Peter.

Notes on the Text
21:17 *the third time:* The repetition of the question for a third time naturally caused Peter's grief, for it reminded him of his threefold denial.
21:19 *by what death he was to glorify God:* Peter, according to tradition, was a martyr, crucified upside down in Rome.
21:20 *the disciple whom Jesus loved:* Most likely John, the youngest disciple and writer of this fourth Gospel.

Peter and Jesus
1. Read John 21:15-22. What same question is repeated three times to Peter in this private talk?
   Why do you think Jesus singled out Simon Peter with this question?
2. What does "more than these" refer to?
   What seems to be competing with Jesus for Peter's love?
3. Love for Christ has to be expressed in action. In what practical ways does Jesus want Peter to express it?
   Who are the "lambs" and "sheep" that Peter should tend and feed?
   What's the difference between tending and feeding?
4. What would it cost Peter to follow Jesus (vv. 18-19)?
   Why does Jesus say "follow me" immediately after he has

indicated that Peter will be martyred?

5. Relate Jesus' command in verse 19 to Peter's question in verse 21. Where does Peter focus his attention?

What does this indicate about a possible conflict in his response to Jesus?

What does Jesus want us to be basically concerned about?

Reflecting on Following *(Choose one)*

6. How many reasons can you think of for why Jesus' disciples should be personally concerned for others?

How can we grow in our love and service for Jesus?

7. Peter had many different things holding him back from total commitment to Jesus. What holds you back? Why?

For further study from InterVarsity Press

How to Begin an Evangelistic Bible Study
Ada Lum tells how Christians can initiate and lead an evangelistic Bible study with their non-Christian friends. paper, 95¢
Jesus the Life Changer
Ada Lum offers eight evangelistic studies in John's Gospel for individuals or groups, directing attention to Jesus as he changed the lives of outcasts and leaders. paper, $1.75
Discussions on the Life of Jesus Christ
Consider the basic message of Christianity, what Christ is like and the implications of his claims. paper, $1.75
Basic Christianity
Margaret Erb provides studies for non-Christians or young Christians on subjects such as the nature of God, the effects of sin and the meaning of belief. Suggestions for leaders are included. paper, $1.75
Out of the Saltshaker
Rebecca Manley Pippert writes a basic guide to evangelism as a natural way of life, emphasizing the patterns set by Jesus. paper, $3.95; study guide, 12 studies, $1.95